GREAT MYSTERIES

The Devil

OPPOSING VIEWPOINTS®

Look for these and other exciting *Great Mysteries: Opposing Viewpoints* books:

GREAT MYSTERIES

The Devil

OPPOSING VIEWPOINTS®

by Thomas Schouweiler

Greenhaven Press, Inc.   P.O. Box 289009, San Diego, California 92198-9009

Library of Congress Cataloging-in-Publication Data

Schouweiler, Thomas, 1965-
    The Devil : opposing viewpoints / by Thomas Schouweiler.
        p.   cm. — (Great mysteries)
    Includes bibliographical references and index.
    Summary: Explores the concept of demonic beings and the question of whether Satan exists.
    ISBN 0-89908-091-X   (alk. paper)   :
    1. Devil—Juvenile literature.   2. Demonology—Juvenile literature.   [1. Devil.]   I. Title.   II. Series: Great mysteries (Saint Paul, Minn.)
BFl531.S346   1992
133.4'2—dc20   92-16424
                                                                        CIP
                                                                        AC

*If the devil doesn't exist, but man has created
him, he has created him in his
own image and likeness.*

Fyodor Mikhaylovich Dostoyevski
1821-1881

Contents

Introduction

This book is written for the curious—those who want to explore the mysteries that are everywhere. To be human is to be constantly surrounded by wonderment. How do birds fly? Are ghosts real? Can animals and people communicate? Was King Arthur a real person or a myth? Why did Amelia Earhart disappear? Did history really happen the way we think it did? Where did the world come from? Where is it going?

Great Mysteries: Opposing Viewpoints books are intended to offer the reader an opportunity to explore some of the many mysteries that both trouble and intrigue us. For the span of each book, we want the reader to feel that he or she is a scientist investigating the extinction of the dinosaurs, an archaeologist searching for clues to the origin of the great Egyptian pyramids, a psychic detective testing the existence of ESP.

One thing all mysteries have in common is that there is no ready answer. Often there are *many* answers but none on which even the majority of authorities agrees. *Great Mysteries: Opposing Viewpoints* books introduce the intriguing views of the experts, allowing the reader to participate in their explorations, their theories, and their disagreements as they try to explain the mysteries of our world.

But most readers won't want to stop here. These *Great Mysteries: Opposing Viewpoints* aim to stimulate the reader's curiosity. Although truth is often impossible to discover, the search is fascinating. It is up to the reader to examine the evidence, to decide whether the answer is there—or to explore further.

"Penetrating so many secrets, we cease to believe in the unknowable. But there it sits nevertheless, calmly licking its chops."

H.L. Mencken, American essayist

Foreword

The Devil in Wisconsin?

(Opposite page) A devil clings to the cloak of a woman he has possessed. The woman seeks a priest's help in church.

In 1908, Anna Ecklund found herself unable to enter the local church. A pious young woman from Wisconsin, she felt as though some invisible force were holding her back. She also felt powerful impulses to attack and destroy the church's holy objects.

Ecklund suffered from these and other strange symptoms for twenty years. Then Father Theophilus Riesinger decided that she was in enough distress to warrant an exorcism, a ritual to free human bodies from possession by the devil or his underlings.

Fearing violence during the ceremony from the possessing devil, the priest decided Ecklund should be restrained. A number of the strongest nuns in the community held her firmly on an iron bed. But when the ceremony began, Ecklund's body flew up and out of the grip of the nuns and landed on the wall high above the door. She hung there with a catlike grip. Great force was needed to remove her from the wall, though no one present could understand how she got there or managed to cling on at all.

As the exorcism continued, events grew stranger still. Ecklund's face twisted and distorted. Her body became so disfigured that she no longer looked like a human being.

In this eighteenth-century engraving, friends and family of a young woman tormented by an evil spirit pray for it to leave her.

Father Riesinger questioned the demon residing in Ecklund and attempted to learn how he might rid her of it.

Priest: How long have you been torturing the poor girl?

Demon: Already since her fourteenth year.

Priest: But that just you, Beelzebub, took possession of her? Who gave you that permission?

Demon: Don't ask so foolishly. Don't I have to render obedience to Satan?

Priest: Then you are here at the direction and command of Lucifer?

Demon: Well, how could it be otherwise?

During the exorcism, the possessing demon seemed to grow quieter and less violent. Still, the end of the ceremony was dramatic.

Ecklund suddenly jumped to her feet. She stood rigid on the iron bed. The priest cried out, "Depart ye fiends of Hell! Begone, Satan!" At this moment, Ecklund's body lost its stiffness, and she collapsed. A terrible screech filled the room. Ecklund opened her eyes for the first time in the course of the ceremony. She smiled and tears of joy rolled from her eyes. Then a terrible odor filled the room. Although the observers opened all the windows, the fresh air did not dissipate the stench.

The exorcism was successful. The demons never bothered Anna Ecklund again.

A Prince of Darkness

What had possessed Ecklund? What caused her to become grotesquely deformed and why did she speak to Father Riesinger with the voice of a demon? What sort of being would inflict such torture on an unwilling and undeserving victim?

The devil, Satan, the Evil One, the Prince of Darkness—people have believed in this being as long as they have believed in a god. Yet, like God, it is a figure cloaked in mystery. Is it possible that a being of pure evil exists? Though not everyone believes in the devil, many people answer this question with an emphatic "Yes!"

One

Where Did Satan Come From?

If asked to draw a picture of the devil, most people would produce a black or red figure who carries a pitchfork, has horns coming from the top of its head, possesses a sinister pointed tail, and looks more like a man than a woman. Few people claim to have seen the Evil One, yet most have this image of him. How did this picture come to exist for so many people?

Satan's Beginnings

Anthropologists seek to understand cultures by looking at the things in the past that shaped and influenced them. By studying the remains of past civilizations, such as writings, art, and objects, anthropologists try to discover how people lived, what they believed, and how their society and culture changed over time. By studying the devil, anthropologists hope to understand what happened in ancient times to cause belief in such a being. Many anthropologists view Satan not as a supernatural force of evil but as a product of human imagination, fear, and superstition.

Many anthropologists believe that the common image of Satan is the result of the merger of two traditions. One is ancient Hebrew theology, the ba-

(Opposite page) In this fifteenth-century woodcut, a horned and clawed Satan (center) and his helpers punish the damned by boiling them in oil.

A prehistoric man draws one of the mastodons he sees nearby. Myths created by early Europeans about unseen forces have contributed to modern conceptions of the devil.

sis for later Christian and Muslim thought. The other tradition developed in the pagan religions that flourished in Europe before the introduction of Christianity.

Pagan Europe

In an essay called "Demons and Disenchantment," anthropologist E.V. Walter said, "Satan grew up in Europe." If the horned, pitchfork-carrying devil can be said to have been born anywhere, he may indeed have been born in Europe, where there is a long tradition of belief in this being. The devil and European civilization were born together thousands of years ago.

Europeans first formed communities about sixteen thousand years ago. They gathered plants and killed animals for food. They made crude clay pots, baskets, and spears. And they tried to make sense of their world.

For early people, the world was a far more puzzling place than it is today. Early people did not understand, for example, what caused disease, what the moon and sun were, or the difference between dreams and waking reality. Because they lacked the scientific information we have today, the world seemed to be a strange place full of mysteries.

Anthropologists speculate that over time, people came to believe there was a connection between their luck in hunting and certain other activities, such as painting animal images on the walls of caves. Such paintings are a common feature of ancient caves. In addition to these painted images of animals, anthropologists have discovered animal claws, teeth, and other body parts fashioned into jewelry by the early people who lived in what we now call France, central Europe, and northern Spain.

This ancient painting, one of the earliest known, was discovered in a cave in France. Scientists speculate that early human hunters drew pictures of their prey as part of a magical ritual to ensure a successful hunt. Such belief in magic was probably the earliest form of religion.

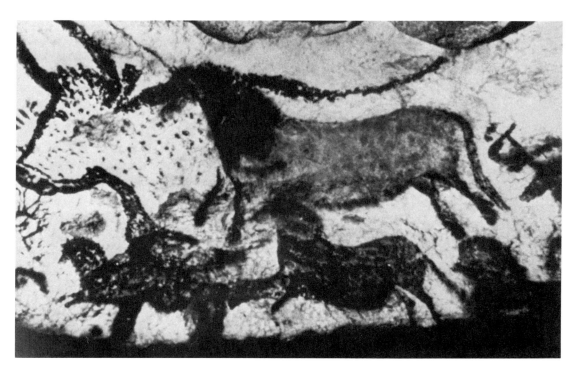

The pieces of jewelry were used as good luck charms, or fetishes, to increase hunting success. The hunters believed that because they had killed such an animal once and now possessed a part of it, they would find it easier to stalk, outwit, and kill another animal of the same kind. In addition, the hunters felt that some of that animal's particular strength would be gained by possession of part of its body. For example, carrying part of a deer's antler would give the hunter some of the deer's speed or agility.

Some anthropologists believe it was this association between luck and the so-called magical properties of fetishes that led to the establishment of religion. Animal fetishes helped the early Europeans feel they had control over their world. Many anthropologists believe that even the most elaborate religions of today are related to these primitive ways of making sense of the universe.

Eventually, the use of animal fetishes for their magical properties became widespread among the early Europeans. Use of fetishes expanded to include the wearing of animal skins, teeth, bones, and horns. As animal fetishes became more common, rituals developed to ensure or increase the potency of the fetish. Magicians whose job it was to oversee these rituals became important.

The Magician's Power Grows

As the magician's role became entrenched in the culture, his—for the magician was most often a male—influence increased. He took over the use of most of the fetishes, and he developed a "uniform" of animal teeth, skins, bones, and horns which he wore on his head.

Soon, the magician was regarded by the people as a supernatural being with extraordinary powers. They believed he had a measure of control over the animal kingdom. They believed the magician also had access to the powers of the dead, who they

An African witch doctor wears the animal skins and feathers that he believes give him power over animals and the ability to communicate with their spirits.

thought lived in an underworld below the surface of the earth. (These early people believed that the world was flat but that it extended infinitely beneath their feet.)

Once the idea of a supernatural being developed, the emergence of the devil was not far behind. The magician of primitive Europe and the devil have some elements in common: both have a special connection to the dead, both have supernatural powers, and both have horns on their head. The figure of the horned man who somewhat resembled an animal, could perform magic, and was associated with an underworld inside the earth, began to take shape. Later cultures adopted the horned, bestial magician figure for their own needs.

Ancient Greece

One such culture flourished in Greece about twenty-five hundred years ago. While the pagan Europeans were developing their culture, the people of Greece were forming beliefs of their own. Greeks of this era, such as Plato and Aristotle, did sophisticated work in mathematics and logic. This work was the basis for much later thought and is still used today. The Greeks also produced a democratic form of government that was later used as a basis for the governments of the United States, France, Great Britain, and other countries.

The Greek people inherited a pagan religion from their primitive ancestors. By this time, however, the religion had expanded a great deal. The Greeks of twenty-five hundred years ago believed in a whole group of gods, called a pantheon. Among the numerous Greek gods were Zeus, the powerful father of other gods and all people; Artemis, a moon goddess and huntress; Demeter, the mother of the earth; and Pan, the god of pastures, flocks, and shepherds.

Pan was an indirect descendant of the horned magician figure. In many ways, he is an exagger-

This statue of Zeus, the ruler of the ancient Greek pantheon, once held a thunderbolt—the god's favorite weapon. Greek religion contributed ideas to Christian concepts of the devil.

Artemis was the Greek goddess of the moon and the hunt. Crowned with a crescent moon and holding her bow, she races across the night sky in her chariot, drawn by two of her servants.

ated version of the horned magician of pagan Europe. Pan was half-human and half-goat, like the primitive magician who dressed in animal skins and appeared to be half-human and half-animal. Pan had the horns of the goat, although the rest of the top half of his body was human. He was hairy, and he had cloven (split) hooves and enlarged sexual organs, reflecting his connection to fertility, sex, and nature. As a god, Pan—like the early European magician—had magical powers and was capable of many superhuman feats.

Another important aspect of Greek religion concerns what happens to people when they die. Their belief is tied to both earlier pagan thought and later concepts of the devil. The Greeks believed that a few lucky souls, primarily royalty and human relatives of the gods, went to a pleasant place called Elysium. All others went to the domain of a god named Hades. This place, also called Hades, was a gloomy and dark place under the ground. Existence there was dreadful and empty. The underworld of

Hades resembles the primitive underworld of the ancient Europeans. Hades himself was the god responsible for bringing death to plants, animals, and humans. He was feared for that reason, just as the devil would later be feared for his powers.

Two recognizable elements of belief in the Evil One began with the beliefs of these early, pagan peoples. The idea of a horned magician and of a dark underworld were further developed and exaggerated by the influential Greek culture. Still, Pan is no Satan, and the realm of Hades is not hell. To understand how these ideas continued to change, it is necessary to look at ancient Hebrew teachings about the nature of God, evil, and the world.

Ancient Jewish and Christian Traditions

The idea of an evil superhuman being—like Satan—emerged as Hebrew ideas about the nature of God changed. Ancient Hebrews, like the Greek people, believed in many gods. This kind of belief is called polytheism. However, over time, Hebrews increasingly began to believe in one all-powerful

In Greek mythology, Hades, the underworld, had a den of punishment known as Tartarus. Three famous inhabitants of Tartarus were (left to right) Tantalus, Sisyphus, and Ixion.

God. In other words, Judaism evolved from a polytheistic religion to a monotheistic one, a religion with a single deity, or god.

God encompassed all things: both light and darkness, both good and evil. At first, the Hebrews saw the devil as a negative aspect of God—His dark side. This view can be seen in the Old Testament of the Bible. For example, in the book of Isaiah, God says, "I form the light, and create darkness: I make peace and create evil. I the Lord do these things." And in the book of Jeremiah, God says, "Behold, I will bring evil upon all flesh." The Hebrews believed nothing could happen that God did not will. Although God was generally kind, He was also capable of evil and He was willing to punish wrongdoers.

As Hebrew theology continued to evolve, God became not only all powerful but all good, a God of love. This belief gave rise to a question that still plagues Judaism, Christianity, and Islam: How can the existence of evil be reconciled with an omnipotent (all-powerful) and loving god? Why does God tolerate evil? Even more troubling, does the existence of evil mean that God is not all powerful? Theologians throughout the centuries have grappled with these questions.

God's Dark Side

At one point in religious history, people believed that evil is caused by a being who is part of God and whose job it is to punish sinners. Later, people came to think that a separate being exists who, though less powerful, is in conflict with God. This idea that God has an evil enemy gained acceptance among Hebrew scholars.

In fact, the word *satan*, from which the proper name Satan is derived, is the Hebrew word for "opponent" or "adversary." This role for the Evil One was incorporated into later books of the Old Testament. For example, Zechariah 3:1-2 reads, "And he showed me Joshua the high priest standing before the angel of the lord, and Satan standing at his right hand to resist him. And the Lord said unto Satan, *The Lord rebuke thee, O Satan.*"

The Bible sometimes shows God and Satan engaged in their eternal contest. For example, in the Old Testament story of Job, Satan challenges God to allow him to test Job's faith. God, believing Job to be a faithful person, allows Satan to torment him. Satan inflicts all sorts of horrible punishments upon poor Job. He destroys all of Job's possessions and covers his body with bleeding sores. Satan, undoubtedly having a good time with all this, is about to kill Job when God stops him. God rebukes the devil for having tempted Him to allow Satan to punish Job for no good reason.

One member of the early Hebrew pantheon of gods was an evil god that lived in the underworld of the dead. As Satan came more to life in the later Hebrew imagination, he became identified with this figure. Eventually, the two became the same being, the devil. Satan's residence in hell officially began. These ideas were generally accepted by Jews by the time Christ was born.

Christianity and the Spread of Satan

The tradition of Satan in hell was accepted and adopted by Jesus' followers, especially those who carried his ideas to Rome and throughout the Middle East. They were, of course, Jews themselves. They were familiar with Jewish theology, and they celebrated Jewish festivals. As founders of the new religion of Christianity, they worked hard to spread their beliefs far beyond the frontiers of the area where Judaism was widely known.

Between the years 400 and 600, Christian missionaries from Rome, the new capital of Christianity, brought their religion to the pagans of Europe, who were still worshiping earth gods and fertility gods in the tradition of Pan. The missionaries spread throughout the continent, rapidly converting pagan

A medieval engraving depicts Job (covered with sores) and his friends debating the justice of his punishment. The Book of Job attempts to answer the question of the existence of evil and its relationship to goodness. In it, Satan and God make a bet on whether Job will remain faithful to God in the face of great suffering.

Europe to Christianity. In the process, most elements of the pagan religions were repressed or extinguished.

But although the Christians wiped out the pagan religions, elements of those religions were incorporated into Christianity. For example, to make the new religion more acceptable, Christians moved the dates of their holy days to concur with certain pagan festivals. Christmas, the anniversary of Christ's

In this illustration from John Milton's *Paradise Lost*, Lucifer, the fallen angel, begins his rule in hell after being cast out of heaven by God.

birth, was moved to the day of the pagan Mithras Sun Feast, the midwinter celebration of the god of light and truth. The Christian holy days became entwined with several pagan traditions. For example, the pagan springtime Ostara festival of fertility, growth, and the resurrection of life became Easter, which celebrates the resurrection of Jesus.

The mixing of the two cultures affected the way the devil was seen as well. Christian missionaries went to great lengths to vilify the old pagan pantheon of gods. They insisted there is only one God. Some pagan gods, however, would not die. One was Pan. He was especially threatening to Christians because he represented sensuality, materialism, and a strong connection to life on earth, values that are contrary to Christian doctrine. Christians therefore tended to identify Pan as a corrupting or evil being. Eventually his image became associated with that of the devil they knew, whom Pan somewhat resembled.

And so the traditions of the pagan horned god and the Judeo-Christian adversary of the Lord met. By the sixth century, the Evil One had taken on the characteristics still recognizable today: He lives in hell, the underworld of the dead. He presides over souls in torment. He is part human and part animal with horns, a tail, and cloven feet. He is connected with magic, he is untrustworthy, and he is a liar. He is the opposite of goodness.

This religious history explains the way many anthropologists believe the idea of the devil came into being. But is the devil merely an idea, a product of the evolution of human culture, a way for people to explain the evil that happens in the world? Many people would say no and argue that the devil is a real being. Belief in such an entity is found around the world today.

"[Medieval Christians believed the Devil had] a human body, the serpent hair of the Greek furies, and a cloven hoof. . . . Satan's trident mocked the triune god. . . . The Devil [was] a hideous blend of repugnant parts, drawing a connection between evil and physical ugliness."

Joannie M. Schrof, *U.S. News & World Report*, March 25, 1991

"[The Devil will be] attractive, nice, and helpful. . . . But bit by little bit, he'll lower our standards where they're really important."

Actor Albert Brooks in the film *Broadcast News*

Two

Satan Around the World

(Opposite page) In his work titled *Apocalypse*, famed fifteenth-century engraver Albrecht Dürer depicted St. Michael and his angels casting Satan and the fallen angels out of heaven and on to the earth.

The devil is real and active in the world right now. This is the conclusion of many different people from different cultures and countries.

Zoroastrians, Christians, and Muslims believe the devil is the supreme commander of all evil in the world and that his powers are matched or exceeded only by God's. Others, such as Hindus, Buddhists, and Native Americans, believe in demons—supernatural beings who cause evil in the world but whose powers are inferior to the devil's. Most people in the world believe in some sort of evil being or beings.

Zoroastrianism

One of the oldest religions in the world to believe in the devil is Zoroastrianism. Also called Mazdaism, Zoroastrianism was founded by the Persian prophet Zarathushtra around 1200 B.C. Once the most popular religion of Persia (modern Iran), it was nearly abolished in its native land during the Muslim conquest of the area in the seventh century. At that time, most remaining Zoroastrians moved to India to escape persecution. Their descendants live there today, where they are known as Parsis, the Indian word for Persians. The Parsis are a small minority in India.

Zarathushtra, also known as Zoroaster, founded one of the world's earliest organized religions, Zoroastrianism. According to the religion, an evil being named Ahriman fights with his equally powerful good counterpart, Ohrmazd.

Zarathushtra believed in two separate spirits or principles, one evil and one good. These spirits originated from a single source called Zuvran, which is beyond good and evil. This view is different from the ancient Hebrew belief that good and evil are inseparable and that evil is simply the dark side of one all-powerful God. Because of this dualism, Zoroastrianism was the first religion with a truly independent devil. Zoroastrians called the evil being Ahriman.

The Zoroastrian creation story begins with two beings separated by a void, an endless empty space. On one side is Ohrmazd, goodness and light, and on the other is Ahriman, evil and darkness. Ahriman, perceiving an existence that is the opposite of his own, seeks to become all-powerful by destroying Ohrmazd. They battle, and Ohrmazd wins and imprisons Ahriman for three thousand years. To celebrate his victory, Ohrmazd creates the universe. He creates vegetation, fire, the primal bull that symbolizes animal life, and the ideal human, called Gayomard.

From his prison, Ahriman longs to bring darkness, lust, disorder, and evil to the world. Because deception is his nature, Ahriman can assume any shape he chooses. He frequently appears in the form of a lion, a snake, a lizard, or a handsome youth. For three thousand years, Ahriman and Ohrmazd struggle for control of the universe. To help him fight, Ahriman creates an evil army of drought, disease, and death, as well as creatures such as vipers and scorpions. Ahriman kills Gayomard.

To counter Ahriman's evil troops, Ohrmazd creates the parents of humankind, Mashye and Myashyane, out of the corpse of Gayomard. He gives them free will, which means they are free to choose whether to follow Ohrmazd's example of goodness or Ahriman's evil ways. They choose to follow Ohrmazd. But Ahriman uses a lie, the essence of evil, to tempt them. As a result, all humans since then have pursued both good and evil.

According to Zoroastrian theology, the end of the universe will come when Ahriman marshals his forces in one last attempt to destroy all creation. But the evil forces, fearing their defeat and annihilation, will turn on each other and be conquered by Ohrmazd. Ahriman will then either be imprisoned or destroyed. Finally, Ohrmazd alone will rule the universe in love and peace.

Zoroastrians assign more power to the devil than the ancient Hebrews did, or even than the Christians and Muslims do. In fact, the only established religion that assigns more power to the Evil One is modern-day satanism.

The Zoroastrian image of the devil had a powerful influence on some later religions. Islam, the dominant religion of the area where Zoroastrianism once flourished, was clearly influenced by Zoroastrianism. Another religion affected by the teachings of Zarathushtra became the dominant religion first of Europe, then of North and South America, Australia, and other parts of the world. That religion is Christianity.

Modern Christian Europe

Although the Christian image of the Evil One is based on the teachings of Judaism, this image changed as theological thought evolved and new cultural forces appeared in Europe. Poets and priests are equally responsible for shaping the idea of Satan accepted by most Christians.

As in Judaism, Satan was originally known as Lucifer, which means "the bearer of light." He was an angel in heaven before the earth was created. Lucifer believed his great beauty surpassed even that of his creator, God. As a result, he believed he was God's equal, and he sat on God's throne. He literally and figuratively put himself in God's place. As punishment, God cast Lucifer down into hell for-

"The Devil does not exist. It is a false name invented by the Black Brothers to imply a unity in their own ignorant muddle of dispersions. A devil who had unity would be a God."

Aleister Crowley, *Magick in Theory and Practice*

"Satan is not a symbol, not a medieval thing of the past. He is very real. He is a being who is consumed by pride and hate and will do anything to keep the mission of Jesus from being accomplished."

Father Emile LaFranz, a veteran exorcist from New Orleans

A fifteenth-century Bible woodcut depicts God casting Lucifer and his angels out of heaven and into the gaping jaws of hell as punishment for their pride.

ever. His temptation of the first humans, Adam and Eve, was Satan's revenge for his divine punishment.

The devil's image was further defined by poets and visionaries in Europe during the Middle Ages, which lasted about one thousand years beginning in the fifth century. They gave the devil a personality in the mind of the common people.

One literary genre, or type of writing, consisted of descriptions of hell and Satan. One of the most famous of these is an eleventh-century Irish work called *The Vision of Tundale*. No one today knows who wrote it.

The Vision of Tundale

Tundale was a greedy and lustful man who became wealthy by lending money and horses to poor farmers and charging high rates of interest in return. One day, while tormenting a poor man for repayment, Tundale received a head injury and fell into a coma. While unconscious, Tundale met a female angel, who took him on a tour of hell. In order to visit Satan, who lived in the very center of hell, Tundale and the angel had to pass by several demons. One was described as

> a beast of unbelievable size and inexpressible horror. The beast exceeded the size of any mountain [Tundale] had ever seen. His eyes were shining like burning coals, his mouth yawned wide, and an unquenchable flame streamed from his face.

While the angel guided Tundale, she made it clear to him that spending an eternity in hell was the fate that awaited him if he continued his corrupt ways.

The tour proceeded, and Tundale encountered another demon who sat atop a lake of ice. It had two wings, a long neck, an iron beak, and two feet with iron talons, with which it snatched up souls to devour. After eating them, the demon excreted the souls onto the ice, where they were revived to receive more torment. Tundale understood that hell was truly a place of unending torment. He begged the angel to return him to the world, but she would not relent. The two pressed on, and eventually they met the Evil One.

> The Prince of Darkness, the enemy of the human race, was bigger even than any of the beasts he had seen in Hell before. . . . For this beast was black as a crow, having the shape of a human body from head to toe except that it had a tail and many hands. Indeed, the horrible

"The new critics argued that Jesus must be seen as a man of his own time. His views were unadvanced, his ideas primitive. When he spoke of the Devil or demons, he merely reflected the superstitions of his day."

Jeffrey Burton Russell, historian and devil expert

"And [Jesus] said unto them, I beheld Satan as lightning fall from Heaven."

Luke 10:18, the Bible

monster had thousands of hands. . . . Each hand, had twenty fingers . . . with fingernails longer than knights' lances, and toenails much the same. The beast also had a long, thick beak, and a long sharp tail fitted with spikes to hurt the damned souls. This horrible being lay prone on an iron grate over burning coals fanned by a great throng of demons. . . . This enemy of the human race was bound in all his members and joints with iron and bronze chains, burning and thick. . . . Whenever he breathed, he blew out and scattered the souls of the damned throughout all the regions of Hell. . . . And when he breathed back in, he sucked all the souls back and, when they had fallen into the sulfurous smoke of his maw, he chewed them up. . . . This beast is called Lucifer and it is the first creature that God made.

The image of Lucifer that so terrified Tundale and his medieval readers contains traditional characteristics of Satan. He has a tail and spikes (instead of horns), and he is part animal, part human. He punishes those who refused to honor God on earth, and so, in a way, administers God's justice. The devil presented in *Tundale* has recognizable elements inherited from both the Judaic and pagan European traditions.

As time passed, however, the image of Satan in Christian Europe changed. This is reflected in a poem written in the early part of the fourteenth century. *The Divine Comedy* was written by Dante Alighieri, one of the greatest Italian literary figures.

Dante's *Inferno*

In *The Divine Comedy*, one section describes hell, Satan, and the nature of Satan's initial sin. Unlike the *Tundale* author, who depicts the devil as a terrifying monster, Dante portrays him as a pitiful figure, forever separated from the warming love of God.

Dante describes how Lucifer had once been the

In his epic poem *The Divine Comedy*, the great fourteenth-century Italian poet Dante Alighieri (below) depicted the devil as pitiful rather than frightening.

highest of angels, a six-winged seraph. Believing he was God's superior, Lucifer took God's throne and was cast out of heaven down to the earth. Lucifer's sin was especially great because of his exalted position in heaven.

In fact, Lucifer was so heavy with the magnitude of his sin that when he hit the earth, the impact opened a great crevasse in the ground and he sank to the very center of the earth. This hole became Lucifer's tomb and hell. During his fall, Lucifer lost his heavenly beauty. His feathery angel wings grew leathery, like a bat's wings. Like the Satan of tradition, he became bestial in appearance, hairy and black with three faces on one head.

Instead of frying on an iron grate, Dante's Satan is permanently frozen inside a vast lake. His wings futilely beat the frozen air, but they will never lift him away. Satan spends all his time chewing three

Marcus Junius Brutus, a Roman statesman, helped assassinate Julius Caesar in 44 B.C. In Dante's *Inferno*, Brutus suffers the eternal fate of being chewed alive by Satan at the very core of hell.

A sixteenth-century illustration from a book about Dante's works shows Dante's three-faced devil munching on Brutus, Cassius, and Judas Iscariot.

Young Martin Luther finds a Latin Bible in the Erfurt University library during his studies there. In his diary, the famed church reformer wrote about his struggles with the devil. The best way to drive away the devil, Luther attested, was to have fun and enjoy life.

famous traitors (considered by Dante to be the worst kind of sinners): Cassius and Brutus, who betrayed the ancient Roman leader Julius Caesar, and Judas, who betrayed Jesus. Blood runs from Satan's mouth and mixes with salty tears wept in frustration.

In Dante's poem, the frozen air of hell is in contrast to the warm, life-giving breath of God. The devil represents coldness, hate, frigidity, and barrenness; God represents the opposite, life and love. Satan is no longer an ogre whose principal duty is to punish humans. He is a being profoundly miserable in his eternal separation from God. Satan is portrayed as being like an animal, although he looks more like a bat or dragon than the Greek god Pan or the Jewish Satan.

Although Dante's portrayal of the devil is more pitiable than past depictions, the Evil One continued to exert a powerful and terrifying influence in people's minds.

The experiences of religious visionaries also helped shape the popular image of the devil. Martin Luther and Saint Teresa were two who encountered the devil personally.

Martin Luther

Martin Luther was a sixteenth-century German theologian whose ideas gave birth to the Protestant Reformation, in which Catholic dissenters formed the first Protestant churches. The Lutheran denomination is named after him.

Luther believed that life is a full-time struggle against the devil. But, he believed, those people who follow the tenets of Christianity can never become the spiritual property of the Evil One. Or, as he put it, Satan's power is "as big as the world, as wide as the world, and he extends from heaven down into Hell"; yet "the evil spirit has not a hairbreadth more power over us than God's goodness permits."

Luther struggled mightily against the Evil One. He kept a journal while he was engaged in biblical studies at Wartburg Castle in Germany. In it, he documented his encounters with Satan. The devil would throw nuts at the roof of the castle and roll barrels down the stairways. He liked to make rattling noises behind Luther's stove. Luther wrote, "He walks with me in the dormitory and he has ordered two devils to keep a watch on me; they are prying devils."

The devil caused Luther to become ill. Luther also documented that the Evil One would grunt audibly and sometimes even dispute theology with him in German. The devil never visibly appeared to Luther, however.

"The important thing is not whether evil is a persona, but that it exists."

Rev. Richard McBrien, chairman of the theology department at the University of Notre Dame

"Rome still holds fast to belief in Satan: in a 1986 sermon, Pope John Paul insisted upon the reality of a personal Devil and recognized the possibility of demonic possession."

Philip Elmer-DeWitt, *Time*, March 19, 1990

Luther said that the best defense against the Evil One is to be busy and happy because the devil feeds on sadness and depression. Luther advocated the enjoyment of food, drink, and other physical pleasures to ward off the devil. He himself would turn to his wife, Katy, when he felt vulnerable to evil influence. Luther promoted exactly the sorts of worldly pleasures the Catholic church believed led humans to evil. Differences like these led Luther to initiate the Protestant Reformation.

Saint Teresa

Though Martin Luther did not see Satan, a nun who lived around the same time did. Like Martin Luther, the Catholic saint Teresa, from Avila, Spain, believed that Satan was constantly working to pervert the goodness of people, especially Christians. She believed the devil visited her frequently in the form of deceit, hypocrisy, and lies. Sometimes, however, he would appear in a physical form. He might appear as a repulsive blotch on her left hand or as a human being who had no shadow and who shot out flames. With a hideously gaping mouth, he would warn Saint Teresa that he was going to possess her. At other times, he would strike her with invisible blows, knocking her to the ground. She wrote: "He rarely presented himself under a sensible [discernible to the senses] form, but very often without any, as in the kind of vision where without seeing any form one sees someone to be present." Teresa could send him away temporarily by sprinkling holy water on him if he was visible or by making the sign of the cross if he was not.

The stories of Martin Luther and Teresa of Avila are significant because they are first-person accounts from people whose honesty and piety were and are respected. Many other tales about the devil fall into the category of folklore, stories that are circulated and probably exaggerated and distorted by frequent retelling before being written down. The

tales told by Luther and Teresa added credibility to the notion planted by people like Dante and the author of *Tundale* that the devil is a very real being.

Dr. Faustus

Indeed, the sixteenth century marks a high point in belief in the devil. Late in the century, an anonymous German Protestant reflected this widespread belief by writing the story of a person who makes a pact with Satan. That person was called Dr. Faustus. Dr. Faustus's story is loosely based on a newspaper account about a student who claimed to have sold his soul to the devil. Faustus's story later inspired other great writers and composers.

Divine Light and the Holy Spirit in the form of a dove inspire St. Teresa of Avila as she writes her famous works on the spiritual life. Teresa reported being attacked physically by the devil.

A seventeenth-century engraving depicts Dr. Faustus standing in a magic circle summoning the devil with magic wand and book of spells in hand.

Dr. Faustus is about a man who was intelligent but vain. He sought knowledge so hungrily that he forgot that because he was human, his knowledge would always be incomplete. He sought to know everything, and he believed it was possible to do so.

One day, while studying a book about alchemy (a mixture of chemistry, magic, and philosophy), Faustus discovered how to summon the Evil One. He did so immediately and made a deal with the devil. He agreed that in exchange for Satan's help in his academic pursuits, he would turn over his soul to Satan at the end of twenty-four years. After the deal was made, the devil took Faustus on a tour of hell. Horrified at what he saw, Faustus wanted to repent, but the devil told him that his sin was too great and that redemption was impossible. This was a lie. But Faustus was a great egotist who believed that everything he did was great. Therefore, he readily believed his sin was too large to reconcile with God, and his arrogance did not permit him to try.

Faustus spent his twenty-four years less in academic matters than in enjoying himself with food, wine, women, and magic tricks done with the aid and companionship of the devil. At the end of his time, Faustus told the story to his students, warning them not to follow the course that he had. During his last night, feeling that his crimes were too vast, Faustus did not repent but went to his room to sleep. At midnight, the students felt a great wind shake the house. Next came a hissing noise and Faustus's screams for help. In the morning, he was found dead on a dung heap with his head twisted around on his mutilated body.

In the story of Faustus, the Evil One seems almost to have become tame. He is no longer a beast ready to tear humanity limb from limb and feast on the remains as he was in the *Tundale* vision. In the Faustus legend, the devil actually becomes a sort of servant to Faustus for twenty-four years before taking him to hell. With the decrease in ferocity, however, comes an increase in cunning. Instead of brute force, the devil uses deceit and special knowledge.

As this lithograph by famed artist Eugene Delacroix illustrates, the devil in the Faustus legend appears in the form of a normal man, not a monster. His power is more intellectual than physical.

He tricks Faustus into thinking he is doomed to go to hell, although according to Christian philosophy, a human is always able to repent before death. By the late sixteenth century, Satan is still as evil as ever, but he operates in a different way.

Though he changed somewhat over time, the devil as seen by Christians in Europe possesses certain consistent traits. Most significantly, he is the master of deceit and lies. He can change shape with ease, appearing as a blotch to Teresa of Avila, as a monster in *The Vision of Tundale*, and as the learned companion of Dr. Faustus.

The belief that deceit is at the center of Satan's existence is also seen in the teachings of Jesus, who told authorities tormenting him: "Ye are of your father the devil, and the lusts of your father ye will do. He was a murderer from the beginning, and abode not in the truth, because there is no truth in him. When he speaketh a lie, he speaketh of his

In this drawing from a nineteenth-century manuscript on black magic, the devil has both the animal-like characteristics of the Greek god Pan and the aristocratic garb of Faust's Mephistopheles.

own: for he is a liar, and the father of it."

Another one of Satan's traits is power. He is able to perform superhuman feats and exert his influence in many places at once. In all of the accounts of the devil, however, he does not have *unlimited* power to inflict his evil on humanity. Satan is not more powerful than God, whose purposes he ultimately serves.

These ideas can also be seen in another religion, Islam, which developed around the seventh century. Islam is the religion of Iran, Iraq, Saudi Arabia, large parts of Africa, and many other places in the world. Its teachings are based on the literature of Judaism and Christianity, but it asserts that both of these religions are superseded by the teachings of the prophet Muhammad, who founded Islam.

Islam

Muhammad was born in Mecca, in present-day Saudi Arabia, around 570. A trading community, Mecca exposed the young man to Christian, Jewish, and pagan Arab thought.

About 610, the archangel Gabriel dictated to Muhammad the contents of a book, the Koran, which became the Islamic, or Muslim, holy book. Jews and Christians believe that their holy books, the Torah and the Bible, are divinely inspired, that God motivated humans to write the words. Muslims, on the other hand, believe God actually spoke to Muhammad through Gabriel and dictated the contents of the Koran to him. Although Muslims respect both the Torah and the Bible, they believe that the Koran is as close to the actual word of God as human beings are capable of understanding.

The Koran teaches that God is totally loving and omnipotent. He has control over everything that happens in the universe. But in Muslim belief, too, there is a devil. The Muslim devil, named Iblis, was originally an angel in heaven, similar to the Christian devil, Lucifer.

Followers of Islam and its founder, the prophet Muhammad, believe in a devil named Iblis who was originally an angel.

Iblis was born the spirit of fire. He lived in heaven at the time God created Adam, the first human, from clay. God commanded all the angels to bow down before Adam, but Iblis refused, believing that a being made of clay was beneath him. Some Muslim scholars view this refusal as an act of extreme piety; they say Iblis's devotion to God did not permit him to bow to anyone but God. But whatever the motive, God expelled Iblis from heaven for his refusal to obey. At the same time, He granted Iblis the right to live on the earth until the day of judgment. On that day, Muslims believe, time will stop. The world and Iblis will be destroyed. Until that day, however, Iblis makes it his duty to tempt humans to evil.

Much like the Evil One in Christian and Jewish belief, Iblis cannot cause humans to sin; he can only tempt them. He tests humans on God's behalf by urging them to go against the teachings of Islam. He urges people to quarrel, to become drunk, to overeat, and to gamble. Iblis is the cause of all sorrow.

As with the devil in the Judeo-Christian tradition, Iblis can change shapes at will. He likes to assume shapes that are pleasing to humans in order to better tempt them.

Demons

Islam and Christianity are two of the largest religions in the world. Along with Zoroastrianism, they are among the few religions today that believe in the devil. Many other religions, however, believe in supernatural demons who are much less powerful than the devil. Demons are generally mischievous spirits who cause trouble or sorrow. Many cultures believe that evil in the world—sickness, crime, and other problems—is caused by a combination of human stupidity and the influence of demons.

While many cultures share the idea that the universe is a place where good and evil coexist, the basis of this evil is often seen differently. Those who

The bodies of seventeenth-century English plague victims are loaded onto a cart to be taken and burned. In medieval times, people thought victims of disease had been attacked by demons.

believe in demons usually see them as personifying specific evils such as extreme heat or cold, disease, insanity, or storms. These beings are not viewed as the personification of all evil. Demons do not possess as much power over the earth as the devil. Most demons of various cultures of the world fall into three categories: trickster, tempter, or punisher.

The trickster is the spirit of disorder and a friend of chaos. It is characterized by childishness, sensuality, foolishness, cruelty, and humor. Its activities

Demons are believed to tempt people to do evil. In this medieval woodcut, a woman falls prey to a demon's temptation to gossip in church during mass.

are more like practical jokes than true evil. Generally, the trickster simply seeks to disrupt the divine order. In Greek mythology, for example, Prometheus upsets the pantheon of gods by stealing fire and giving it to humanity.

Some demons play the part of the tempter, as the devil does in Islam and Christianity, prompting human beings to commit evil. In Buddhist teachings, the god Mara (whose name means "death" or "thirst") is the father of desire, unrest, and pleasure. He is a demon whose attributes are blindness, murkiness, death, and darkness. One story of the Buddha, the holy person for whom the religion is named, tells that Mara tried to obstruct the Buddha's path to enlightenment by tempting him with the pleasures of this world. Another example of a tempter demon is found in the beliefs of the Toltecs of Mexico. They believe an army of demons offered

Quetzalcoatl, a being that is part human and part god, red wine and other enticements to distract him from his religious duty.

Demons who are punishers most resemble the devil. This kind of demon helps God by punishing humans who deserve it. For instance, the ancient Egyptians believed that demonic spirits tormented the souls of the dead for a period of time before they moved on to paradise. In Japan and China today, some people believe demons punish human beings who have angered the gods in some way. As in Western thought, it is not quite clear whether these demons are employees of God, willingly performing his commands, or inmates in God's prison—hell—forced to do his bidding.

Three

Who Are the Devil's Worshipers?

Some people not only believe in the existence of the devil but worship him as well. They choose to align themselves with the powerful forces behind the evil in the world. Today, there may be as many as 100,000 practicing satanists around the world.

Satanism in the Middle Ages

Satanism is not new. It is believed to have originated in Europe in the Middle Ages, when Christians from Rome were spreading their religion across pagan Europe. Those who rejected the new religion continued to practice their old pagan rituals. Over time, Christianity became such a dominant force that the pagan practices were continued as a rebellion against Christianity rather than as an alternative religion. The pagan participants increasingly embraced Satan, the figure who represented the total rejection of the Christian way of life.

As paganism turned into satanism, many practices emerged that are still seen today. Male and female witch doctors were descendants of the horn-wearing witch doctors of the ancient pagan tribes. They used their magic against their Christian persecutors rather than to heal the sick or help ensure good luck during a hunt. Witches used their energy to cast spells against Christians. Naturally, they

"A growing number of horrifying crimes is being committed under the rubric of Satanism. . . . Drug and child-selling networks run by the occultists have recently come to the attention of law enforcement agencies. . . . At least one investigator believes Satanism to have an international component as well."

National Review, book review of *Cults that Kill: Probing the Underworld of Occult Crime* by Larry Kahaner

"There is no national Satanic conspiracy, and credible sources report that there is very little ritual abuse [physical harm due to satanic rituals] occurring."

Publisher David Alexander in *The Humanist*, May/June 1990

sought out the Christians' worst enemy to help them.

Many rituals of the early satanists represent a perversion, or corruption, of the practices of Christianity. The most famous of these is the Black Mass, an inverted version of the Catholic church service. During a Black Mass, the Lord's Prayer was recited backward. Praises to Satan, instead of God, were read. Spells were cast on enemies or on those the caster of the spell wished to influence. Sex or bloody sacrifice were frequently involved to demonstrate a connection to and respect for Satan. The ritual of the Black Mass continues in some satanic circles to this day.

Once the "church" of satanism was established, ex-pagans were not the only people involved in its rituals. Superstitious Christian peasants, fearful of both the nobles who ruled them and of the elements of nature, sometimes dabbled in satanic practices in an attempt to appease both God and the devil. Aristocrats, seeking adventure, practiced Black Masses and other satanic rituals to increase their worldly power and to take part in the sexual freedom of satanism.

Satanism in medieval Europe, though never truly widespread, was nonetheless strong enough to endure to modern times. Interest in satanism was reborn in the nineteenth century, when it moved to the United States.

Modern Satanism

One form of satanism visible in modern America first came to the attention of authorities during the last century in extremely rural areas in the Ozark Mountains of Arkansas and Missouri. Here, certain women were reputed to have magical powers, and they gained reputations as witches. Most of these women were so-called "white witches," working against evil by removing spells and curses for clients or curing disease. However, tales were circulated about a band of witches who worshiped the devil and practiced black magic. Stories of their practices showed the influence of older European satanism.

It was believed that these witches met in cemeteries by moonlight. A woman wishing to join the society of black witches was to hang her clothes on the tombstone of an infidel, a bad Christian. Having done this, she was to renounce her Christian teaching and swear allegiance to the devil. She then had sexual intercourse with a male representative of Satan while the other witches stood in a circle and chanted to attract the attention of the devil. Then, the Lord's Prayer was recited backward.

This ceremony was repeated on three consecutive nights. Up until the third night, the initiate was allowed to back out. After the third pledge, however, she was forever bound to Satan.

These stories have been passed down by an illiterate and uneducated people who would not have read about the European satanism of old. Scholars

Two modern satanists perform a ritual at a shrine in their home. Many satanic symbols are just inverted religious or magical emblems, like this inverted pentagram.

In the early twentieth century, New York magician Aleister Crowley became famous for his dramatic ritual performances and his promotion of sexual freedom. His writings influenced later satanists.

therefore believe that satanic practices were brought to the United States by European immigrants. These practices existed only in very remote areas until the early twentieth century.

Aleister Crowley

During World War I, rumors of satanic activity sprang up in New York City. These rumors were related to the arrival of a magician and showman from England whose name was Aleister Crowley.

Crowley's main concern was magic, not satanism. However, he employed many satanic symbols and rituals in both his magic and his self-developed religion, which he called Crowleyanity. He referred to himself as "the Beast 666," which is a symbol for Satan found in the book of Revelation in the Bible. His beliefs had more to do with magic than with either God or the devil, in which he did not believe. Crowley believed in the magical power of sex and love, which is an element of satanic theology. He was best known for his strange and mystical magic ceremonies held in New York City. Crowley influenced later generations of satanists. His flamboyant display of magic, his theories about free love and sex, and his use of occult symbols set the stage for a reawakening of interest in satanism that took place in the United States in the late 1960s, a time of widespread social rebellion.

Anton LaVey and the Church of Satan

The practice of satanism in the last half of the twentieth century owes a great deal to an organ player and animal tamer who was born in Chicago in 1930. Anton Szandor LaVey is the founder of the Church of Satan, which claims to have around seven thousand members and has several chapters in operation in the United States and Europe. While satanic activity today is not confined to members of the Church of Satan, this is the best known of all satanic organizations.

All potential members of the Church of Satan must pass rigid screening procedures. Applicants must attend three indoctrination lectures, complete a written examination on the function and nature of the church, and participate in an interview with an inner circle of church members.

Like other churches, the Church of Satan is based on a book. In this case, it is *The Satanic Bible*, written by LaVey. More than 618,000 copies have been sold since its publication in 1969, year three of the Satanic Age, according to LaVey.

Satanic Commandments

In *The Satanic Bible*, LaVey explains the guiding principles of the church. LaVey and other satanists believe that the devil represents strong emotions, such as the powerful love and hate experienced by all people. Through the expression of these powerful emotions, people may channel their energy into purposeful, meaningful action. Religions like Christianity, satanists believe, do human-

Anton LaVey and followers perform a ritual in their satanic church in 1967. The church, located in San Francisco, follows the teachings of LaVey's *The Satanic Bible*.

ity a disservice by attempting to repress certain strong emotions. This repression reduces the power and potential for fulfillment in each individual. The value placed on experiencing strong emotions and feelings can be seen in the Nine Satanic Statements, which is almost an inversion of the Ten Commandments of the Torah and Bible:

1. Satan represents indulgence, instead of abstinence!

2. Satan represents vital existence, instead of spiritual pipe dreams!

3. Satan represents undefiled wisdom, instead of hypocritical self-deceit!

4. Satan represents kindness to those who deserve it, instead of love wasted on ingrates!

5. Satan represents vengeance, instead of turning the other cheek!

6. Satan represents responsibility to the responsible, instead of concern for psychic vampires!

7. Satan represents man as just another animal, sometimes better, more often worse than those that walk on all fours, who, because of his "divine spiritual and intellectual development," has become the most vicious animal of all!

8. Satan represents all the so-called sins, as they all lead to physical, mental, or emotional gratification!

9. Satan has been the best friend the church has ever had, as he has kept it in business all these years!

The nine statements and other satanic writings from the Church of Satan show that this branch of modern satanism is more concerned with rejecting Christianity and enjoying the earthly pleasures of life than with actively pursuing violence and evil.

Anton LaVey's philosophy attracted many followers, and the church flourished. Popular enter-

A number of Hollywood celebrities, including talented entertainer Sammy Davis Jr., once experimented with the satanic practices of LaVey's church.

tainers like actress Jayne Mansfield and singer Sammy Davis Jr., experimented with LaVey-style satanism. In 1969, however, a charismatic and mentally ill young satanist named Charles Manson and his followers killed pregnant actress Sharon Tate and six other people. This grisly murder turned public opinion against satanism, although the Church of Satan actually does not advocate violence.

Today, LaVey lives in a thirteen-room house in San Francisco, California. He continues to practice his version of satanism. Not all people claiming to be satanists follow the tenets of the Church of Satan that he founded, but all satanists today must acknowledge the important part LaVey has played in reigniting interest in satanic philosophy.

Different Kinds of Satanists

Many experts see differences in the level of commitment people have to the worship of the Evil One. Modern analysts divide devil worshipers into four general categories: intergenerational cults, satanic churches, self-styled satanists, and experimental satanists.

The least is known about the first group. Members of these small and secretive cults are born into them. Outsiders cannot join. Because of the high level of secrecy, no one knows how many of these intergenerational cults exist.

Satanic churches, which are entitled to the same government protections and benefits in the United States that are accorded other churches, emerged and gained their widest popularity during the cultural upheaval of the 1960s. The Church of Satan is the best-known example of such an organization, although it is not the only one.

Another satanic church is the Temple of Set, named after an Egyptian god of evil. This organization is led by Michael Aquino, who was a friend of LaVey's until they quarreled about the practice of devil worship. Satanists, according to Aquino, are

Satanist Charles Manson and four of his followers ritually murdered actress Sharon Tate in 1969. Their crazed violence and lack of remorse turned a once-tolerant public against satanists.

Demented serial killer
Richard Ramirez, California's
Night Stalker, displays an
inverted pentagram tatooed
on his palm. The symbol is
commonly associated with
satanism.

not people bent on violence. They are people who worship themselves as entities separate from the rest of the universe, and who work "for the good of humankind."

Self-styled or secondhand satanists embrace the superficial elements of satanism. They use traditional satanic symbols and words to express the psychological demons within themselves. For example, in 1989 Richard Ramirez, known as the Night Stalker, was sentenced to death in California for killing more than twelve people. Ramirez, who was deeply disturbed, drew pentagrams on the walls of his victims' homes. The pentagram is a five-pointed star inside a circle. It is considered a symbol of satanism the way the cross is a symbol of Christianity and the six-pointed star is a symbol of Judaism.

The fourth group, experimental satanists, is probably the largest. These are mainly teenage males whose activities range from short-term dabbling in satanic philosophy to the murder of animals and, in some rare cases, people. Psychologists believe that satanism is appealing to many young people who feel they are not in control of their lives. Satanism promises that the devil will deliver power to them. They look at the war, disease, famine, murder, and child abuse in the world and conclude that evil is stronger than good. By participating to some degree in this evil, they feel, they can also participate in the power it represents.

Increasing Signs of Satanism?

Some authorities say that in recent years, signs of satanism have been appearing at increasing numbers of crime scenes. In the desert about twenty miles east of El Paso, Texas, there is a pit where satanic ceremonies are carried out. It contains the mutilated carcasses of dogs and cats, probably kidnapped from residential areas. In the woods near Chicago, authorities have found animals hanging from trees, "666" written on tombstones, and altars smeared with blood.

This devil's-head jacket was worn by a high school student who stabbed three schoolmates in a suburban Chicago school in 1988. Teens often adopt satanic symbols and practices as ways of rebelling against society. Some, like the owner of this jacket, carry it too far.

These cauldrons and bowls were used by a satanic cult in Mexico that murdered twelve people in the late 1980s. Most satanists claim that their religion is nonviolent and that violence is done by those who are not true satanists.

One former satanist, now a born-again Christian, is Ed Mitchell* of Tennessee. He reports that at the age of eleven, he was recruited into a cult of about two hundred people. Three years later, on the night of the first full moon of March, he was fully initiated into the group. He lay down on a slab of cement and let the satanic high priest cut a gash deep into his leg. "If Lucifer heals you," the priest told Mitchell, "you will become one of us. If not, you will die." During the ceremony, the group, called a coven, danced in a circle around him.

* These names have been changed.

Ed Mitchell survived and embraced the life of a satanist. As part of his ritual, he first sacrificed rabbits by picking them up by the ears and slicing their throats. Later, Mitchell says, he ate human flesh obtained through a mail-order catalog. When a person is a satanist, "All your feelings are in reverse. Terror is exciting; feeling good is an abomination," Mitchell said. He stayed with the cult for six years before breaking away and seeking psychological help. Today, he counsels other teenagers who are trying to give up satanic practices.

Other former satanists say that ritual killing is only a small part of satanism. The primary interest of most satanists is philosophy. Peter Francis* says that satanists worship in much the same way as members of all religions do. He states, "I didn't do a lot of animal killing or drinking blood. That's a misconception. When people think of Satanists, they think of the Charles Manson type. When [satanists] worship, they do it all in the mind and try hard to follow what their church says. The difference is, we tried to do what the *Devil* says."

"Investigators . . . kept hearing these stories [of Satanism]. . . . Then in 1985 stories of ritualized abuse began to surface, and we in the police began to take notice. These children all tell similar stories, describe similar events."

Sandra Daly Gallant, a seventeen-year veteran with the San Francisco Police Department who has been investigating cults since 1978

"In four years . . . investigators have found no evidence that cults are preying on the nation's children."

The Commercial Appeal, a magazine published in Memphis, Tennessee, in a series about child abuse

Four

The Devil's Clutches

(Opposite page) An illustration depicts a story of possession from the Gospel of Mark. The evil spirits within the possessed man made him so strong that he could not be restrained, even with iron chains.

In 1906, a young woman named Claire, who was a member of the Bantu tribe of Natal, Africa, cried out in the night. The walls of the Catholic mission in which she lived echoed with her cries: "I am lost! My confession was sacrilegious! My communion was sacrilegious! I shall hang myself!"

A few days later, she appeared more tormented than ever. She gnashed her teeth and barked like a dog. She called out to one of the nuns at the mission, "Sister, send for Father Erasme. I want to confess everything. Quickly, quickly, the Devil wants to kill me! He's my master." Claire passed a note to Father Erasme, saying that she had sold her soul to the devil.

At first, the mission staff believed Claire was suffering from a mental illness, but her behavior soon made them believe otherwise. Claire refused to participate in the sacraments, Catholic ceremonies that signify allegiance to the faith. Horrified, Claire pushed away all holy objects, saying that they burned her.

More important, Claire knew of events that she could not have known about, events that had occurred in places and times she had never visited, events not well known to anyone. Claire had very

little education, yet she understood questions put to her in many languages, including Latin, the traditional language of the Catholic clergy. In fact, she suddenly knew Latin religious ritual better than the staff of the mission did. She corrected the priests when they made a mistake. These and other aspects of Claire's behavior convinced them that the devil was inside Claire, directing her actions and speech.

Claire's devil was talkative and seemed to enjoy revealing the most intimate secrets of the mission staff and other people around Claire. A mention of Jesus or the Virgin Mary enraged him.

Sometimes, the devil would act upon, rather than through, Claire. For instance, he would lift her in the air despite efforts by many people to hold her

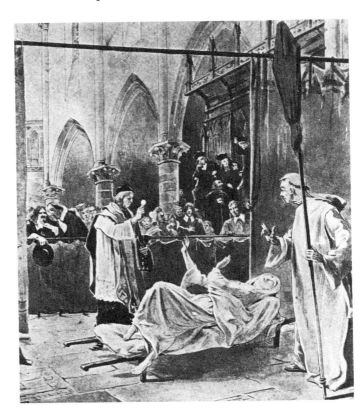

A woman possessed by a devil undergoes an exorcism in a medieval church.

down. He would inflate her stomach or make her head grow in size. At other times, a lump would appear and travel around her body. Claire would also drop to the ground, writhe, and stick out her tongue like a snake. All these symptoms would disappear if she was sprinkled with holy water, which is the blessed water used by Catholics to perform rituals of cleansing and baptism.

An Exorcism

Bishop Henri Delalle, a high-ranking official in the Catholic church, decided that another kind of ceremony needed to be performed: an exorcism. An exorcism is a ceremony performed by a holy person to force the devil or devils to leave the body of a possessed person. In the Catholic church, a special order of priests, the Jesuits, was founded in 1534 to be teachers. Considered spiritually superior to normal clergy, they were specially authorized to perform exorcisms, although all Christians may perform them. In Claire's case, a church leader was brought in to remove her devil.

Claire's exorcism took place in front of many people. It began with two and a half hours of prayer. Suddenly, Claire levitated six feet from the floor of the church. While she was suspended in the air, the devil seemed to call out from her body to the bishop, "What's the matter, Bishop? Why do you have to stand there gaping at me? Do as I do!" Then Claire cackled an unearthly laugh. Eventually, the exorcism was completed successfully. Claire behaved normally and acted as a model Christian until her early death six years later.

The exorcism performed on Claire is a ceremony developed by the Christian church. It originates in a command by Jesus that his followers "drive out devils" in the world. The ceremony itself probably began to take shape shortly after his death around A.D. 35. Most of the ritual that survives today dates back one thousand years.

"There's a lot of confusion about the Devil. You can't arrive at what he is by reason. Reason cannot demonstrate either his existence or nonexistence. Why? Because the Devil is a spiritual being and spiritual beings are not the fruit of reason."

Monsignor Corrado Balducci, scholar of demonology

"Satan is a symbol, nothing more. He's a symbol of [humankind's] carnal nature—[its] lust, greed, vengeance, but most of all [its] ego. Satan signifies our love of the wordly and our rejection of the pallid, ineffectual image of Christ on the cross."

Anton LaVey, founder of the Church of Satan

An exorcism, unlike many rituals and ceremonies of the church, does not depend on a rigid formula. Rather, the exorcism is developed from a set of general instructions. They are adapted to the circumstances of each particular case. Throughout the ritual, dialogue with the possessing devil is expected to dictate in part what happens during that exorcism. It is not always the devil himself who does the possessing. Sometimes a demon in Satan's service possesses the victim.

The Exorcist's Ritual

The person performing the exorcism must have permission from a bishop of the Church and must be a person of piety and integrity. The possessed person prays and fasts in the tradition of Jesus before the exorcism and should hold a cross or have a cross in front of him or her. The priest must take care that any holy items used to weaken the evil spirit are not damaged by it. The possessed person is generally tied down if the demon within is prone to violent outbursts.

The priest begins the ritual by invoking protection from God for himself, his assistants, and the possessed person by making the sign of the cross and sprinkling holy water. He then recites a prayer asking for deliverance from sin for all of humanity. After this is done, he summons the spirit inside the possessed. He begins by saying,

> Unclean spirit! Whoever you are, and all your companions who possess this servant of God . . . tell me, with some sign, your name, the day and the hour of your damnation. . . . Do no damage to this creature [the possessed], or to my assistants, or to any of their goods.

If the possessing devil responds, the exorcist may proceed by asking questions. The exorcist may ask the name of the possessing spirit and try to discover when and why it entered the possessed. He may also ask how the spirit entered the possessed

A woodcut depicts a medieval Roman Catholic bishop. As spiritual head of a region called a diocese, the bishop must give permission before any exorcism can be performed in the name of the church.

person—through occult activities or a sorcerer's spell, for example.

The next step is to read from the Bible. The excerpts read are Jesus' teachings on the power of God over the devil.

After the exorcist is satisfied that he has all the information he needs, he addresses the evil spirit and commands him to leave the body of the possessed. The command begins:

> I exorcise you, Most Unclean Spirit! Invading Enemy! All spirits! Every one of you! In the name of our Lord Jesus Christ: be uprooted and expelled from this creature of God. He who

In this Renaissance painting, a priest exorcises a demon from a possessed woman. The small figures above depict the power of the priest's spirit driving away the demonic spirit.

commands you is he who ordered you to be thrown down from highest Heaven into the depths of Hell.

As the ceremony continues, the exorcist calls Satan "the primeval adversary, the ancient enemy of Earth, [who] surrounds [the possessed] with the horror of fear, paralyzes his [or her] mind with darkness, strikes him [or her] with terror, agitates him [or her] with shaking and trembling."

At the end of the exorcism, the exorcist commands Satan to leave, saying, "Leave therefore now. Go away. Seducer! The desert is your home. . . . Be humiliated and cast down. . . . [God] you. All things are subject to his power: He has expelled you."

The ceremony is concluded with an expression of faith from those present, readings of more religious texts, and a prayer of thanks.

An exorcism may not be successful the first time. Often, an exorcism must be performed many times before the possessed person is at peace. Although the exorcism was originally performed in Latin, it can be given in any language. Exorcism of the devil in Christianity dates back to the original teachings of Jesus.

The Jews had a long tradition of performing exorcisms. The book of Acts in the New Testament

An evil spirit throws a man to his knees as Jesus (left of center) drives it out.

"[Catholic Cardinal O'Connor] revealed to reporters that priests had been authorized to perform two exorcisms in his archdiocese over the past year [1990]. 'As far as we know,' he said, 'they have been successful.' "

Philip Elmer-DeWitt, *Time*, March 19, 1990

"[So-called demonic possession] provides a means of casting off authority for, once possessed, a man is no longer responsible for his actions. . . . Secondly, it provides a method of projecting any doubts or guilt feelings held by the person tormented."

Arthur Lyons, *The Second Coming: Satanism in America*

describes Jewish religious leaders roaming the desert and casting devils out of possessed people. Jesus, as a religious leader, continued in this practice. In the New Testament books that tell the story of his life, one passage describes how Jesus cast the devil out of a possessed man.

Biblical Stories of Possessions and Exorcisms

Jesus had been traveling and teaching. Landing by boat in the land of the Gerasenes, he was immediately confronted by a man who ran up to him, fell at his feet, and asked, "What do you want of me, Jesus, son of the Most High God? Swear by God you will not torture me!" This was a strange statement for the man to make, especially since Jesus was not yet well known as the Messiah, God's son.

Further, the man himself was unusual. Originally from a nearby village, Decapolis, he moved to some hills in the desert where the tombs of the dead were kept when his behavior grew too strange for his fellow villagers. The villagers had attempted to tie him down, but he would break even strong chains when he became agitated.

Jesus immediately replied, "Come out of the man, unclean spirit. What is your name?"

"My name is legion," came the answer, "for there are many of us." (*Legion* was a term that referred to the Roman army; it meant "several thousand" or "a great many.") The spirits inside the man begged Jesus not to send them back to "the abyss," or hell, but rather into a herd of pigs nearby. Jesus consented, and the pigs immediately charged down a cliff into the lake where they drowned.

Afterward, the man sat on the sandy ground, calm and "in his full senses." He asked Jesus if he could go with him, but Jesus told him instead to return to Decapolis and tell of his experiences.

In another story, Jesus was traveling with his followers when they came to a town where a troubled man told Jesus that his son was possessed by

"a dumb spirit," a spirit that prevented the boy from speaking. The father told Jesus that the spirit also caused his son to tremble and to fall to the ground, even in water or in fire, and to become rigid and grind his teeth. These things had happened to the boy since he was a small child. Furthermore, the father had asked Jesus' disciples to cast out the evil spirit, but they were unable to do so. The father was afraid that his son would hurt himself. He was also afraid of the devil who he feared possessed his son.

Jesus sent for the boy, who immediately began to convulse when he saw Jesus. He writhed on the ground and foamed at the mouth.

"Deaf and dumb spirit," said Jesus, "I command you: come out of him and never enter him again." The boy's convulsions grew worse, and then he was still, so still that the people gathered around thought he was dead. Jesus, however, took the boy by the hand, helped him up, and took him into his house.

Jesus exorcises a man possessed by devils. Most people of Jesus' time believed that the ability to cast out devils was a sign of divine power and authority.

When asked about the spirit that possessed the boy, Jesus told his disciples that this kind of spirit can be removed only by prayer.

Possession in Piacenza

Stories of demonic possession continued to be recorded during the next two thousand years. Especially in the past two centuries, many possession cases were recorded as scientists, priests, and philosophers attempted to make sense of them. One particularly chilling story is that of an Italian woman who was first told that she was insane.

In May 1920, a small woman presented herself to Friar Pier-Paolo Veronesi at the church in Piacenza, Italy. She asked the friar for his blessing. Shy at first, the woman told him about strange and fearful things that were happening to her. At certain times, a force would take control of her and cause her to dance, against her will, for hours at a time, until she dropped from exhaustion. She would sing songs that she had never heard and give lectures to an unseen audience in a language she did not know. She told the friar that she often had the urge to destroy, to bite to pieces any object that she held. She had torn almost all of her husband's clothes to shreds. At other times, she would jump from chair to chair or hop up onto tables, while roaring, barking, screaming, and meowing. She was terrified by these experiences, partly because she could not control them and partly because she would be bruised for days afterward.

She told the priest that receiving a blessing would prevent the episodes from occurring for a few days. Seeking such help, she had once tried to go to a church whose priest was said to be particularly gifted in helping people ward off evil spirits. But her horse stopped before reaching the church and refused to go further, even though the coach driver whipped it bloody. Then, she told the friar, she jumped from the carriage and began to fly about two feet from the ground in the direction of the church. When she found herself back on the ground, she rushed inside and received a blessing, after which she felt better.

Friar Veronesi received permission from his bishop to exorcise the woman's demon. The first exorcism took place on May 21, 1920, in a room on the first floor of the friar's church. Besides the woman and the friar, the woman's husband, mother, friend, and two other ladies were present. A doctor also stood by in case he was needed.

Friar Veronesi began the ceremony, intoning the Latin text: "*Exorcizo te, immundissime spiritus, omne phantasma, omnis legio.*"

When she heard these words, the possessed

A sixteenth-century woodcut depicts a woman's struggle against the evil spirit who tries to possess her.

A demon is expelled from a possessed woman in answer to the prayer of St. Catherine of Siena (d. 1380). Jesus promised his followers power over evil spirits.

woman jumped from her chair with extraordinary agility and landed in the middle of the room, her face twisted. She screamed insults at the friar. Then she said, "And who are you, to come and fight with me? Do you know that I am Isabô, that I have great wings and strong fists?" After saying this, she again screamed insults at the friar.

Seven Years of Possession

Though Isabô continued his abusive ways, the friar questioned him. Friar Veronesi learned that Isabô had great power, that he had companions in his possession of the woman, and that he had entered her body on April 23, seven years before. He had entered her body when she ate some salt pork that a sorcerer had cast a spell over. Isabô stated that he would not leave until the woman vomited this meat she had eaten seven years earlier!

During the course of the exorcism, Friar Veronesi sprinkled holy water on the woman. This caused her to throw herself down and writhe on the floor. When the friar placed one end of his garment on the woman's shoulder, Isabô yelled, "Get that weight off me!"

The exorcism continued until the friar and the possessed woman were exhausted. After making Isabô promise not to harm the woman or her family, the friar ended the ceremony.

He performed ten more exorcisms on the woman, but still Isabô would not leave her body. By the last exorcism, however, Isabô showed that he was tiring. He no longer spoke through the woman's mouth but through small and weak signals he made with her hands. Still rebellious, he told the friar that he would not leave before June 23, 1920.

On that day, the twelfth exorcism began. The friar began the event according to the ritual and then addressed Isabô. "In the name of God," he cried, "I command you to obey me in everything. Do you understand?" There was no reply.

"If you have understood, raise one arm: if not, raise two." One of the woman's arms rose slowly, as if by great effort.

By such signs, the friar learned from Isabô that the other devils had already left the woman's body. The friar spoke: "By all the authority given to me by God, I command you, foul spirit, to come out of this body immediately. If you come out at once I will send you into the desert, into the center of the Sahara: *If not, I will send you back to Hell!*"

The woman moved slowly. She pushed back the thick black hair that fell into her face. Tears filled her eyes. Looking bewildered, her muscles slack, she said in a low, mournful voice, "I am . . . going." She lowered her head into a nearby basin and vomited a great deal of matter.

"Go! Go!" cried the friar.

Suddenly, the woman cried out in her own voice, "I am cured!"

The doctor and Friar Veronesi examined the contents of the basin. At the bottom was a piece of salt pork, about the size of a walnut, with seven small horns.

Karen Kingston

Born to an alcoholic father in 1960, seven-year-old Karen Kingston witnessed this man brutally slay her mother with a butcher knife. She sank into a state of shock and did not recover. Withdrawn and morose, she was placed in a foster home until she began to throw violent fits. Then, in January 1969, she was turned over to the North Carolina state authorities. They placed her in a home for retarded children.

There, her condition deteriorated. Soon, Kingston could no longer feed or care for herself. She could not read or write, and her IQ was considered to be below 50. (Average intelligence is rated at 100.) Her hair turned from reddish-brown to a coarse and dull color. She grew pale, and she developed pimples and running sores. Her body gave off a foul stench.

Three years after entering the home for retarded children, Kingston lost her good posture and became extremely stooped. Her eyes were crossed. One leg had become shorter than the other. Medical doctors were perplexed; they did not understand what caused Kingston to look more like a sickly old woman than a young adolescent.

Robert Pelton, an investigative writer studying the phenomenon of demonic possession, suggested an exorcism. Despite skepticism on the part of many staff members at the home, the procedure was carried out on April 13, 1974, by the Reverend Richard Rogers; his wife, Ruth; Father John Tyson of the Catholic church; and Donald Sutter of the Baptist church. A clinical psychologist, a psychiatrist, a medical doctor, and three nurses observed the event.

The procedure began at 7:00 A.M. with readings from the Bible by Rogers. He then ordered the evil spirits to leave the possessed girl.

Immediately, a mocking reply came from Karen Kingston's mouth: "This girl is mine! Go away! Go away! She belongs only to me! Leave us alone!"

Stunned observers looked at each other in silence. Rogers continued: "What is your name, you creature of death and destruction?"

Kingston replied in a deep male voice, "I don't have to tell you anything! You are too weak to make me do anything. I *own* this girl. This girl is mine. *Only mine!*"

Rev. Trevor Dearing, an Anglican priest, exorcises evil spirits from a young woman during a special service held in 1975 at St. Paul's Church in Hainault, England. Though not as common as in the ancient world, occasional possessions do occur in the modern, civilized world.

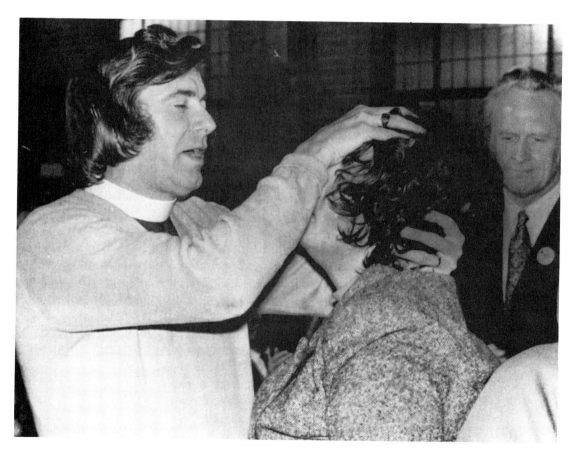

Father Henri Gesland, a French Roman Catholic priest, was appointed official exorcist for Paris in 1968. In six years, he had thousands of cases brought to him. He considered only four to be actual cases of demonic possession.

Rogers coaxed the possessing spirit to write something on a piece of paper. After first refusing to do so, Kingston picked up a pen and wrote a paragraph in longhand script. The nurses from the home were shocked; they knew that Kingston was, on her own, incapable of writing anything.

Rogers then began to pressure the spirit, commanding it to leave Kingston's body. She screamed, "I'll come, but I'll kill this [girl] first!"

Robert Pelton, in his book *The Devil and Karen Kingston*, describes what happened next:

A faint tinge of bluish-green color appeared to [come] from Karen. It enveloped her completely like a cloud. There no longer was any doubt about it—the aquamarine haze slowly changed to a dynamic red-orange followed by a brilliant flash of blinding light.

Karen tensed, screamed, and catapulted from her chair. . . . [The spirit] came forth with a roar like a wounded bull. The sound was deafening. And then [it] left on Rogers' command to return to where [it] had originally come from. Karen ceased to quiver. The room was quiet.

At this point, Ruth Rogers noticed that Kingston's hair had returned to its former shiny and soft state. After the exorcism, Kingston regained the physical and mental condition of a normal teenage girl. Her legs were the same size, and she no longer limped. She stood straight. Her IQ jumped to 74 a week after the exorcism and by two years later had increased to 110, above average.

Work of the Evil One?

Claire, the Gerasene man, the boy who could not speak, the afflicted woman from Piacenza, and Karen Kingston: Was the devil using their bodies as a temporary home to do his evil work? Does Satan really enter the bodies of unsuspecting humans to injure them and take them away from God?

There are many who say it is silly to attribute such things, bizarre as they might be, to a supernatural force like the devil. They look to more earthly causes.

Five

How Do Skeptics Explain the Devil?

Few people dispute the existence of evil in the world, but many do not believe in either devils or demons. Some people think the devil is a projection of the evil and shame each person carries inside. Others do not believe in any sort of supernatural being, God or the devil. They do not regard demonic possession, for example, as proof that the devil exists. They have other explanations for this phenomenon.

Carl Jung

Carl Gustav Jung was a Swiss doctor in the early twentieth century. He developed a theory that states that human behavior is explained in part by the influence of culture. Jung's ideas remain very influential today. Among his many ideas, Jung proposed the existence of something he called the collective unconscious.

He based this idea on the repeated occurrence of certain symbols in the art, literature, and everyday thought of people in many different cultures and in many different times. For example, the sound of thunder makes people from many different kinds of backgrounds think they are hearing the voice of a god, though their religions are not the same.

(Opposite page) In the early 1970s, Rev. Christopher Neil-Smith was authorized by the bishop of London to conduct exorcisms. Here, he demonstrates the technique he uses on possessed children. Most of his subjects were rebellious teenagers who needed counselling more than exorcising.

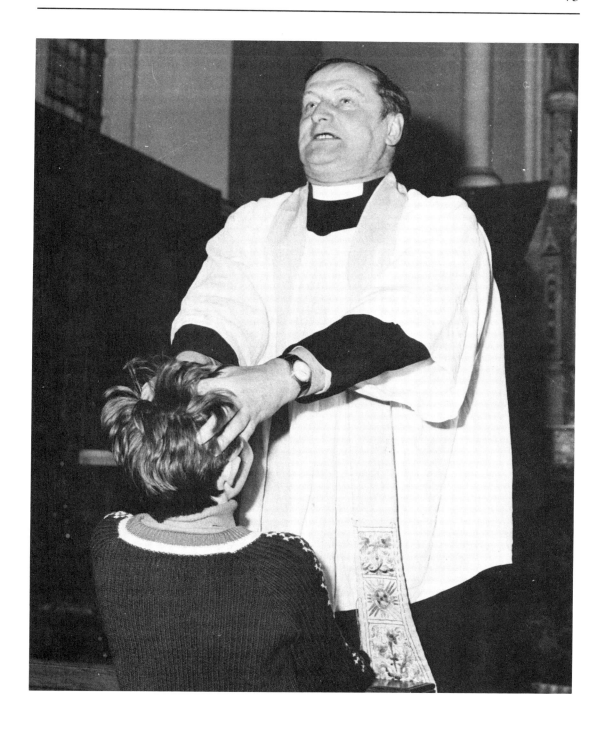

Swiss psychiatrist Carl G. Jung theorized that the devil is an imagined entity onto whom humans project their own unexplainable evil impulses.

When he realized that people from diverse cultures interpret many phenomena similarly, Jung proposed that certain ideas about the world are universal, common to all people. These shared ideas and reactions are a result, he said, of the past experience of the human species. The experiences of our common ancestors are somehow built into our brains, into our collective unconscious. This is what makes us respond to certain events in similar ways.

Jung believed the idea of the devil is a result of the collective unconscious. He also theorized that all people feel impulses that they believe are evil. People react the same way to these feelings by externalizing, or placing outside themselves, the negative feelings. They remove the evil from themselves and transfer it to an outside being. In Christian, Muslim, Zoroastrian, and ancient Hebrew belief, the being that embodied the evil of humanity, Jung said, was called the devil. Other peoples placed the negative feelings into similar beings such as evil spirits or multitudes of demons. The beings are slightly different, but the idea is the same.

Therefore, Jung would argue that Martin Luther was really encountering his own feelings of evil when he thought he was interacting with the devil. *The Vision of Tundale*, Jung might say, is simply a story in which a man expresses in a dream his own negative feelings about his selfishness and greed. The devil, according to Jung, is a part of each of us that we do not want to admit we have.

Atheism

Atheists also do not believe the devil is a real being. Atheists believe there are no supernatural beings like God, the devil, and demons. Although almost all people used to believe in some sort of god or supernatural force, many people do not today. Of Americans polled in 1990, 31 percent said that they did not believe in God, the devil, heaven, or hell. Jeffrey Russell, a scholar who has written a great deal about God and the devil, put it this way: "In society as a whole . . . belief in the existence of both God and Devil has drastically declined since the eighteenth century . . . because of the growing predominance of materialism." In other words, the ideas of God and the devil do not fit into the modern world as well as they fit the times of *Tundale* or *Faustus.*

Atheism has existed for many centuries, but most scholars agree that its current popularity began in the eighteenth century with the rapid scientific advancements of that time. As science explained many of the mysteries of the natural world, such as how plants and animals came to exist, old religious ideas about the creation of the world came into question. As these ideas were replaced, people began to wonder if other religious ideas, such as the existence of God and the devil, were also unreliable.

"With the educated middle classes, there is a rapid decline in the popular belief in the Devil and demons from roughly 1800 onward."

Jeffrey Burton Russell, historian and devil expert

"Satan does not have God's power, but he has far more than we [humans] do—even the power to work miracles."

William D. Eisenhower, Presbyterian pastor and adjunct professor at Fuller Theological Seminary

As scientific and atheistic ideas spread, the devil came to be seen as an example of the absurdity of traditional religious beliefs. Even some Christian theologians, who still firmly believed in the existence of God, abandoned the devil. They said that when Jesus spoke of the devil or demons, he was using the terms of his times. He did not necessarily believe in the devil's literal existence as a being who could be spoken with or seen.

Today, very few theologians believe in the devil as a being who can threaten them personally. In-

Jesus encounters the devil as a person. Many people today, including some theologians and satanists, do not believe that the devil is a person.

stead, they see the threat arising from the abstract notion of evil. They have more fear of muggers than of the devil. Many people accept this view. Even some practicing satanists agree, saying that the devil is just a metaphor for the strong impulses within people.

Some, however, say that demonic possession is certainly proof that the devil exists. But those who do not believe in the devil have several possible explanations for so-called possessions.

Hoaxes

Some possessions are clearly hoaxes. Take the case of Marthe Brossier, who lived in France during the late sixteenth century. She exhibited the signs of possession. She attacked a friend and accused her of having ruined her hopes for marriage. Brossier's belly swelled, and several times her body bent back so far that her head touched the ground. During these times, she would shout, "I am more tormented than if I were in hell!"

Brossier was taken to see doctors and religious experts, and they concluded that she was possessed. When exorcised, she did not understand the questions in Greek and Latin that were put to her as most possessed persons are able to. Her body shook, and she mocked the exorcist. The exorcist, however, concluded there was "nothing demonic, not much illness, [and] a great deal of acting."

Marthe Brossier later admitted her hoax. She had acted as if she were possessed, but she never really believed the devil was inside her.

In some cases, even the victim does not realize the possession is a hoax.

Aldous Huxley was a British novelist and essayist who expressed skepticism about demonic possession. One symptom of possession he particularly questioned was the knowledge of an ancient or foreign language. Huxley believed that the supposedly possessed person had heard the language some-

Twentieth-century British thinker and writer Aldous Huxley rejected demonic possession as proof that the devil exists. He believed such phenomena could be scientifically explained.

where or had known it as a child. He wrote:

In the cases where [possessed] persons . . . have shown a . . . knowledge of some language of which they were consciously ignorant, investigation has generally revealed the fact that they had spoken the language during childhood and subsequently forgotten it, or that they had heard it spoken and, without understanding the meaning of the words had unconsciously familiarized themselves with their sound. . . . In the light of what we know . . . it seems questionable whether any alleged demoniac [possessed person] ever passed the test of language in a completely unambiguous and decided manner. What is certain is that the recorded cases of complete failure are very numerous, while the recorded successes are mostly partial and rather unconvincing.

Huxley thought that "possession" was poor proof of the devil and that alleged demonic behavior could generally be explained logically.

Advances in humanity's understanding of the world, especially in areas like medical science, also call into question the idea of demonic possession. Perhaps the pain suffered by people undergoing such possession has more earthly origins.

Physical Disorders

The advance of medical science has made understandable some things that were once mysterious. For example, only a few hundred years ago, many people believed the moon caused some people to become insane. Today, scientists understand that mental illness is caused by a variety of social and medical problems and that the moon has nothing to do with it.

Remember the boy who could not speak upon whom Jesus performed an exorcism? His symptoms were typical of many possessions: He felt fine until an episode began. Then his personality changed, and he began to shake until he fell to the ground, rigid. He would grind his teeth and be unable to speak.

This boy's symptoms were very like those caused by a physical disorder modern doctors know as epilepsy. Epilepsy is a disorder of the brain, spinal cord, nerves, and nerve centers, which is characterized by the tendency to have recurring seizures. Epilepsy affects about 2 percent of all people. Julius Caesar, the Buddha, Napoleon, the painter Vincent van Gogh, and *The Divine Comedy*

In this illustration, Job's wife berates him for his stubborn refusal to blame God for his suffering as the devil afflicts his body with sores. In the ancient world, many physical diseases were attributed to supernatural beings.

The great French general Napoleon suffered from epilepsy, a disease with symptoms similar to those described in some possession cases.

author, Dante, were epileptics.

The types of seizures epileptics suffer vary in intensity. The most severe, called grand mal seizures, include many of the symptoms of possession. The seizure begins with strange or irritable feelings for a period of hours or even days. Then the person becomes rigid, often falling to the ground and frequently losing consciousness. Following this phase, convulsions begin in the arms and legs or throughout the entire body. Frequently, the mouth will open and close, and sometimes the person will bite his or her tongue. After this, the convulsions subside and consciousness returns, but the epileptic remains confused, drowsy, and stiff for hours afterward. Even if the person remains conscious throughout the seizure, he or she may not remember the experience.

Some scholars argue that most historical "possessions" were, in fact, the symptoms of diseases like epilepsy for which the ancient people had no explanation or cure.

Understanding Disease

In his book *The Devil, Demonology, and Witchcraft*, Henry A. Kelly argues that in ancient times, superstitious people considered all illness to be the result of infestation by evil spirits. As people came to understand the nature of disease, this idea became less widespread. It was still used, however, especially to explain things that were not understood. The causes of epilepsy, for example, are still not fully understood today, and effective treatment was not developed until the twentieth century. Witnessing an epileptic seizure with its violent behavior and change in personality makes it easy to understand why people used to attribute it to the devil.

Like epileptic seizures, the behavior of the men-

The Romans of Julius Caesar's time would probably have interpreted his epileptic seizures as a sign that he was possessed, not by a devil, but by a god.

tally ill can be strange and frightening to those who do not understand what the afflicted person is undergoing. That is why scholars believe that many behaviors diagnosed in the past as demonic possession were really the actions of the insane.

Sybil was an unhappy French girl of the nineteenth century who was tortured by images of the devil. She told a priest that as she was about to fall asleep, the devil would come to her bed, strip her of her physical body, and carry her spiritual "double" body into a celestial sphere. Here, he would amuse himself by torturing her. He wounded her with heavy blows, whipped her, threw her into bushes of thorns, and even fired bullets through her spiritual double. She would beg him to return her to her body, pleading until she was exhausted. Then he would return her. Sometimes she would try to move her body while the double was outside of it, and she would stumble and fall to the floor of her bedroom. During these occasions, Sybil would observe strange things, such as objects in the room moving and bending.

Sybil believed she was possessed by the devil. She tried to keep him away by sprinkling holy water around her bed and by wearing a religious symbol. In biblical times, many people would also have believed she was tormented by the devil. But the priest she spoke with did not believe she was possessed. Instead of performing an exorcism, he sent her to a hospital in Paris where she spent many months. She was diagnosed as mentally ill and was successfully treated.

Many Explanations

Many scholars argue that it is likely that people who seem to be possessed by the devil are actually suffering from the effects of physical or mental illness. These afflictions are better understood today than ever before and therefore can be recognized and treated.

"Satan is God. . . . He is all the elements interwoven in what we call evolution."

Anton LaVey, founder of the Church of Satan

"[People] caught up in the demonic drama of spiritual warfare are tempted to attribute to the demonic [that] which is actually due to personal, moral irresponsibility."

Bob and Gretchen Passantino, *When the Devil Dares Your Kids*

A young girl, naked and insane, crouches in an empty asylum room. Though few today attribute the cause of madness to demonic possession, mental illness is still very much a mystery.

Science has done much to undermine belief in the devil. Its explanations of the universe have cast doubt on religious views of the world. An understanding of physical and mental illness has explained many supposed possessions of the past. Together, science and atheism have virtually proved that there can be no such thing as the devil. Or have they? The nineteenth-century French poet Charles Baudelaire wrote, "The Devil's deepest wile is to persuade us that he does not exist."

Afterword

Does Satan Exist?

(Opposite page) A robed worshiper of nature—a pagan—cries out to his god. Humans appear to have a need to reach out beyond themselves to something—or someone—perceived to be more powerful than they are.

Though many are skeptical about the existence of the devil, many others assume that he is real. The number of satanic cults attests to this fact. In addition, in 1989, 12 percent of teenagers answering a *Seventeen* magazine poll indicated that they had "some or a lot of faith" in satanism. Other polls indicate a recent rise in such beliefs. A Gallup poll taken in November 1991 indicated that more people—about 7 percent—believe in hell and the devil than in 1965. Most of the people expressing this belief were young, between the ages of eighteen and twenty-nine.

Interest in the Evil One can be seen in popular culture, as well. During the 1970s, rock musicians Ozzy Osborne and AC/DC explored satanic themes. This tradition is continued today by the little-known King Diamond, who shares his stage with an altar and a coffin. Other, better-known bands like Slayer and Venom, also use demonic images in their music.

The devil has been seen in a lot of films as well. *The Exorcist* series deals with demonic possession, and in *The Omen* series, the devil is born on earth and eventually becomes president of the United States. In the most famous film with a satanic theme, *Rosemary's Baby*, Anton LaVey himself

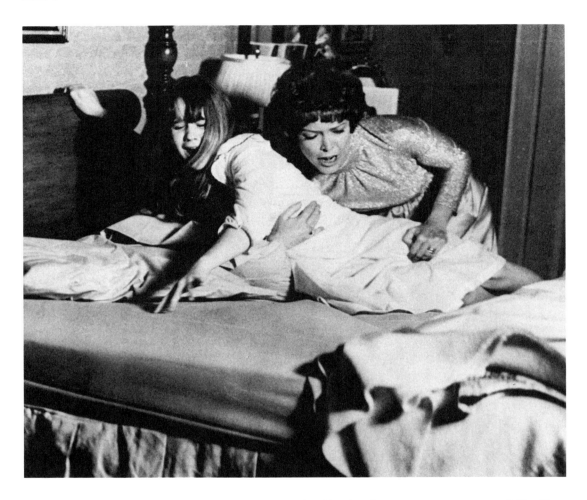

A scene from *The Exorcist*. Demonic possession has proved to be a popular motion picture topic. The magic of cinema has made the devil very real for some people.

plays the devil who impregnates actress Mia Farrow. Countless talk shows deal with a supposed satanic crime wave sweeping across the nation.

Does all this mean that the devil exists?

There are many different ways of seeing the Evil One. Perhaps the devil is just a symbol for the negative and violent impulses that reside inside each human being. Maybe Satan is a phantom, an idea that grew out of pagan Europe's hunting cults and developed as they were replaced by Christianity. Maybe there is no devil.

It is equally possible that Satan does exist. No argument against his existence proves absolutely that he is the product of human imagination. Jay Anson, an author who investigated strange occurrences at a house on Long Island, New York, reflected that even the strangest events cannot prove the existence of the devil. Yet, he writes, "Any other hypothesis immediately involves us in trying to construct an even more incredible series of bizarre coincidences, shared hallucinations, and grotesque misinterpretations of fact." Indeed, the witnesses to the exorcism of Karen Kingston, intelligent members of the twentieth century, would find it difficult to come up with a better explanation for what they all saw.

For Further Exploration

Jay Anson, *The Amityville Horror*. New York: Simon & Schuster, 1977.

Natalie Babbitt, *The Devil's Other Storybook: Stories and Pictures*. New York: Farrar, Straus & Giroux, 1987.

Natalie Babbitt, *The Devil's Storybook: Stories and Pictures*. New York: Farrar, Straus & Giroux, 1974.

F. Forrester Church, *The Devil and Dr. Church*. San Francisco: Harper & Row, 1986.

Adam Crabtree, *Multiple Man: Explorations in Possession and Multiple Personality*. New York: Praeger, 1985.

Lawrence Wright, "It's Not Easy Being Evil in a World That's Gone to Hell," *Rolling Stone,* September 5, 1991.

Works Consulted

David Alexander, "The Devil *Didn't* Make Her Do It," *The Humanist,* May/June 1990.

Barry L. Beyerstein, "Neuropathology and the Legacy of Spiritual Possession," *The Skeptical Inquirer,* Spring 1988.

Léon Cristiani, *Evidence of Satan in the Modern World.* Translated by Cynthia Rowland. Rockford, IL: Tan, 1974.

Paul Edwards, editor in chief, *The Encyclopedia of Philosophy.* Vol. 8. New York: Collier Macmillan, 1967.

Philip Elmer-DeWitt, "No Sympathy for the Devil," *Time,* March 19, 1990.

Jane Furth, Mimi Murphy, et al., "Satan," *Life*, June 1989.

Aldous Huxley, *The Devils of Loudun.* New York: Harper & Row, 1952.

Henry Ansgar Kelly, *The Devil, Demonology, and Witchcraft.* Garden City, NY: Doubleday, 1968.

Nina Killham, "Satanism," *Seventeen,* August 1990.

Anton Szander LaVey, *The Satanic Bible.* New York: Avon Books, 1969.

Marcel LePée, "Saint-Thérèse de Jésus et le démon." In *Satan, the Early Christian Tradition,* by Jeffrey Burton Russell. Ithaca, NY: Cornell University Press, 1981.

Jean Lhermitte, "Pseudo-Possession." In *Soundings in Satanism,* assembled by F.J. Sheed. New York: Sheed & Ward, 1972.

Wayne Lutton, "The Right Books," *National Review,* October 28, 1988.

Arthur Lyons, *The Second Coming: Satanism in America.* New York: Dodd, Mead, 1970.

Malachi Martin, *Hostage to the Devil: The Possession and Exorcism of Five Living Americans.* New York: Reader's Digest Press, 1976.

Michael G. Mauldin, "The Life and Times of the Prince of Darkness," *Christianity Today,* August 20, 1990.

Rodney Mearns, ed., *The Vision of Tundale.* Heidelberg, Germany: Carl Winter Universitetsverlag, 1985.

Bob Passantino and Gretchen Passantino, "The Kingdom Strikes Back," *Christianity Today,* November 11, 1991.

Robert Pelton, *The Devil and Karen Kingston.* Tuscaloosa, AL: Portals Press, 1976.

Carl A. Raschke, *Painted Black.* New York: Harper & Row, 1990.

Adolph Rodewyk, *Possessed by Satan: The Church's Teaching on the Devil, Possession, and Exorcism.* Garden City, NY: Doubleday, 1975.

Jeffrey Burton Russell, *The Devil: Perceptions of Evil from Antiquity to Primitive Christianity.* Ithaca, NY: Cornell University Press, 1977.

Jeffrey Burton Russell, *Lucifer, the Devil in the Middle Ages.* Ithaca, NY: Cornell University Press, 1984.

Jeffrey Burton Russell, *The Prince of Darkness: Radical Evil and the Power of Good in History.* Ithaca, NY: Cornell University Press, 1988.

Joannie M. Schrof, "The Devil's Metamorphosis," *U.S. News & World Report,* March 25, 1991.

Richard Lowe Thompson, *The History of the Devil: The Horned God of the West.* New York: Harcourt, Brace, 1929.

Bill Turque and Farai Chideya, "The Exorcism of Gina," *Newsweek,* April 15, 1991.

U.S. News & World Report, "Hell's Sober Comeback," March 25, 1991.

E.V. Walter, "Demons and Disenchantment." In *Disguises of the Demonic.* New York: Association Press, 1975.

Index

AC/DC, 86
Adam, 40
Ahriman
  as Zoroastrian devil figure, 26
  story of, 27
alchemy
  as way to summon the devil, 36
Alexander, David, 46
Alighieri, Dante, 30
Amorth, Father Gabriele, 66
anthropologists
  studies of ancient civilizations, 15, 16
  studies of Satan, 12-14
Aquino, Michael, 51-52
Aristotle, 17
Arkansas, witches in, 46-47
Artemis, 17
atheists
  devil theories of, 77

Balducci, Corrado, 59
Baudelaire, Charles, 85
Bible, 39
bishop
  as capable of exorcism, 60
Black Mass, 46
Brossier, Marthe
  demonic possession of, 79
Brutus, 32

Cassius, 32
Catholic church, 34
Christianity, 20, 24, 44
  origin of Satan and, 14
  spread of, 21-23
Church of Satan, 51
  description of, 48-50
Claire
  exorcism of, 59-60
  tale of demonic possession of, 56-59
collective unconscious
  devil as emanating from, 76-77
Crowley, Aleister, 48
cults
  intergenerational, 51

Davis, Sammy, Jr., 51
death
  Greek concepts of, 18-19
Delalle, Henri
  exorcism of, 59
Demeter, 17
demonic possession
  as proof of devil's existence, 79
  case history of, 66-69
  example of, 56-59
  hoaxes, 79-80
demons
  religions that believe in, 24
devil, 11
  belief in today, 86
  categories of, 42, 43
  Hebrew origin myths of, 19-20
  origins of, 17
  pagan elements of origin, 23
  skeptics' opinions about, 74-85
  tormentor of Martin Luther, 33-34
  worshipers of, 44-55
    categories of, 51-52
  see also Lucifer; Satan
Diamond, King, 86
Divine Comedy, The, 30-31

Ecklund, Anna
  possession of, 8-11
Eisenhower, William D., 77
El Paso, Texas
  satanic practices in, 53
Elysium, 18
epilepsy
  explains early demonic possessions, 80-83
Europe
  as origin of satanism, 14, 44
exorcism
  definition of, 59
  description of, 60-63
  example of, 66-69
    Anna Ecklund, 8-11
    Karen Kingston, 70-73
  performed by Jesus, 64-66
Exorcist, The, 86

About the Author

Thomas Schouweiler was raised in Marine on St. Croix, Minnesota. He received his bachelor's degree in English language and literature from the University of Minnesota. He has worked in numerous occupations, including librarian, produce stock person, paralegal, and restaurant worker. This is his third book in the Great Mysteries series.

Picture Credits